WHAT HAVE THE IMMIGRANTS
EVER DONE FOR US?

PROVOCATIONS

WHAT HAVE THE IMMIGRANTS EVER DONE FOR US?

KELVIN MACKENZIE

WITH RESEARCH BY
BRHMIE BALARAM

SERIES EDITOR:
YASMIN ALIBHAI-BROWN

Biteback Publishing

First published in Great Britain in 2015 by
Biteback Publishing Ltd
Westminster Tower
3 Albert Embankment
London SE1 7SP
Copyright © Kelvin MacKenzie 2015

ISBN: 978-1-84954-841-0

10 9 8 7 6 5 4 3 2 1

A CIP catalogue record for this book is available from the British Library.

Set in Stempel Garamond

Printed and bound in Great Britain by
CPI Group (UK) Ltd, Croydon CR0 4YY

Contents

Part I

Part I

The University of Life

I GREW UP in Camberwell in the 1950s post-war era – an age of passing austerity and regeneration. People forget that the '50s were a time of great change. In terms of possessions and lifestyles those days were unimaginably different from our times, but, at a deeper level, there is continuity between then and now. Camberwell in the nineteenth century had grand Georgian and Victorian houses and also workers who had left the countryside to find jobs in the city. Then it went through one of those cycles: affluent people moved on or out, and it became more tight-knit working class. Now, the high end of south London is colonised by luvvies and professional, rich, young entrepreneurs, and the big houses are selling for insane amounts of money, pushing up other house prices. But you still have small buy-to-let properties and council houses. Like everywhere in our cities, there is a varied population in terms of class, race, ethnicity and income. This has always been the case. It is not a recent phenomenon.

When I was growing up, Bermondsey was almost entirely white and working class – kinship and all that. The residents stuck together, looked after each other and didn't even like white people from elsewhere. It was a fortress mentality. But the fortress would, of course, crumble. Camberwell had a different history and profile. Charles Booth, the Victorian do-gooder, made a poverty map of London in 1889.[1] He was a wealthy businessman who wanted to uncover the real facts about the indigent in the capital. He found that in and around those leafy streets, the truly abject lived adjacent to the well-off. It was not a community and the poor did not have it easy, but there were no unapproachable ghettos or gated compounds.

---

1   In 2012, the BBC revisited Booth's research and showed what Camberwell was like over 100 years ago. You could see how much had changed, but also how cycles repeat themselves.

And that is how it was during my childhood. Those big people in big houses lived very different lives but were in the same space as us. Kids played hopscotch in the streets, many with sooty faces and uncombed hair. (The same kids would be pristine when they were going to school. Education was valued, teachers respected.) Mums and dads worked hard, wanted better, had dreams.

My parents were both journalists – my father edited the *South London Observer* and my mother was the chief reporter. Journalism is in my blood. My mother was incredibly industrious – like so many women were then and are today. She'd be out all day in the police courts, reporting council matters, attending inquests and getting stories. Then she would come home, make dinner and clean the entire house. We lived in an upscale council flat near Ruskin Park. In my family we always debated and discussed what was happening, which meant that from a young age I was aware of world politics and domestic affairs.

That block of flats had only white residents, but I remember a guy called Mohammed, whose father was a doctor at University College Hospital. I used to clean cars on the estate and he paid me to wash and polish his car. As I grew up, we started to get used to seeing different skin colours. A few Afro-Caribbeans moved in. What I remember most about them was their style. It was particular. The men wore suits and hats of a different variety to the locals – they were elegant and stood out – and I didn't look at the women (boys didn't do that). The availability of relatively inexpensive housing stock in Camberwell was the draw for these newcomers. There really wasn't too much concern about the new arrivals. It was just part of the flux and swing of life. In Camberwell, unlike Brixton, we didn't get a large, sudden inflow.

By the early '60s, the government had embarked on a project to build high-rises. Nowadays, these tower blocks are hated, but back then they were loved by the working classes. The Scottish novelist Andrew O'Hagan lived in one of those flats. For his family, after the damp, awful tenements in Glasgow, these buildings that reached to the skies felt like a release and a real advancement. People begged to get onto the waiting lists for these properties.[2]

---

2   *Evening Standard*, 8 July 2009.

The Ruskin Park estate was a cut above the rest. The trade union leader Jack Jones lived there for many years. I essentially grew up in a neighbourhood that had all classes in it, as well as mobility.

Estate agents today describe Camberwell as:

> A typical London mix of large supermarkets, nail bars, phone and chicken shops. The famous arts school gives it a creative edge, while its fine Georgian houses, popular with actors, writers and lawyers, live cheek by jowl with social housing. The big houses sell for £2–3 million.[3]

Why does this matter? Because it reminds us that Britain, though at heart a conservative nation, never stands still. It is restless and shape-shifting. From that comes hope and energy.

Let us consider Brixton's history since the war. A wave of workers came in from the Caribbean and the locals were taken aback. Some streets soon had only

---

3 *Evening Standard*, 14 August 2014.

Afro-Caribbeans. White flight seemed to hasten this process. I worked in Brixton for a while at a bookmaker's and saw this happening. By the early '80s this inner-city area was seen as an almost entirely black zone. The riots that took place when Margaret Thatcher was Prime Minister seemed to represent a racial protest – a sign of a troubled and alienated place.

More than fifty years on, Brixton has gone up, is a des res address and has people from every background. The people – working-class white and minority groups – who bought their homes in the '60s have made a phenomenal capital gain. The same is true in Notting Hill – another area of poverty and migration. Alan Johnson's autobiography describes what it was like back then, with ruthless landlords and habitations not fit for rats.[4] Look at it now. The black and white people on basic wages who managed to buy and do up run-down properties in the '60s have made a pile. The PM and millionaire Russians own houses there and it has gone posh. That is the inevitable circulation of demographics, income and

4   *This Boy*, Corgi, 2014.

economics. It is the British way, geographically and culturally, too. Roast beef loses to chicken tikka masala and then comes back into favour. Or maybe Thai green curry does. It is who we are; how we are. Today Camberwell is much more multiracial and varied than in my day.[5] So are Salford, Bath, Glasgow and all our city spaces.

In the US, supposedly *the* socially mobile country, housing is firmly segregated along income lines as well as race lines. That has not changed in spite of Obama being in the White House. As we all know, fortunes and lives are determined by the possibilities of escape. That is harder in America than we think and they claim. In the UK, no ward is composed entirely of one race and there is a natural ease between various peoples. It is no accident that the UK has the highest number of mixed-race families in the western world. In fact, biracial children have been under-counted by statisticians. According to the BBC's Mark Easton, who has looked at the figures, around two million people in Britain are

---

5 See Ole Jensen on Bermondsey and Camberwell, based on research for the think tank Compas: compasoxfordblog.co.uk/…/integration-and-neighbourhood-relations

mixed race, 'therefore a larger group than any of the defined "ethnic minorities"'.[6]

I lived in New York in 1978 and was astonished by how cosmopolitan it was. Yet, go back there now and you'd immediately realise London has become the cosmopolitan capital of the world. Everyone just gets on – it doesn't matter whether you are walking down a flashy road in Mayfair or a side street in Edgware where a whole bunch of Arabs are sitting outside smoking their bubble pipes.

And it goes way beyond London. You see Koreans in north Surrey – they work for Samsung or other companies. The number of French migrants to the UK has increased every year since 1991 – in parts of Somerset and Dorset the French have small businesses and you can see them at food markets. Diversity is just everywhere. Kate Middleton invited her local Indian corner shopkeeper Chan Shingadia and his wife to her wedding to our future king. Moeen Ali, a Muslim cricketer with a long beard, plays for England – well, prays and then plays.

---

6   'Britain More Mixed Than We Thought', BBC online report, 6 October 2011.

What this all proves to me is that nothing stays the same – society is changing at 2,000 miles per hour – and that the future will bring more movement, energy and variety. This is the future we must embrace.

I have been phenomenally lucky. Indeed, most of us born after the Second World War have been lucky. There have been no wars involving myself or my family and we haven't suffered any plagues or famines. As I get older, I do think about that. I was raised in a country that gave me free education and healthcare. And since then, that country has steadily got wealthier. Sometimes I think we need to remember how fortunate we have been.

But nothing stays the same. Nothing can. Nothing should. Not areas, not nations, not individuals. That is perhaps the meaning of life. As I get older, I am also more puzzled about things – more curious, more questioning. Many of the 'things' we hold dear turn out to be absolute cobblers. Some people are too set in their ways.

People should learn their own history. Do they know that Isambard Kingdom Brunel – the celebrated engineer who created the Great Western Railway, constructed important bridges and built Paddington Station – was of

French heritage? Eddie Izzard, too, is descended from Huguenots (French Protestant migrants). We would have no Stephen Fry or Marks & Spencer without Jewish migrants, who were also persecuted by the people of this country. We would have no Lewis Hamilton, the demon racer, and we would not have won all those medals at the 2012 Olympics without athletes like Mo Farah and Jessica Ennis. We cheer them when they win for our nation but still continue to bash migrants and minorities. It does not make sense. And it is unfair. People – whatever their colour, religion or culture – all strive for the same things: they want their kids to thrive; to be safe, productive and respected. It's what we all want. I never understood this before but, as I have gone into the real world, I've thought more deeply and learnt some basic truths.

And one big truth is this: our country would come close to not functioning at all if we did not have minorities. Just think of the GDP and their contribution to it. There are so many examples. Take Euro Garages. In 2001, two brothers, Mohsin and Zuber Issa, bought a small, nearly derelict petrol station in

Bury, Lancashire. Their father had worked in a garage and the boys loved forecourts. Even through the deep recession, their business grew phenomenally and today they have seventy-three garages and an annual turnover of £300 million.

Similarly, the Poles who used to clean and build for us now run their own companies. Public institutions, the service sector and small businesses all need migrants. Ugandan Asians arrived in 1972 after Idi Amin threw them out. They came, they saw and they knew they would become economically successful. An acquaintance told me a story of how, when placed in re-settlement camps provided by the British government, these exiles who had lost everything were soon full of verve and plans. They had walked the streets and seen that grocery shops shut at 5 p.m., so they found a niche: 'We will be rich. We will stay open longer and get rich. These guys here can't work as hard as we can.' And many did get rich. They were resented when they came and are resented now because they have made it. Minorities, for many Britons, are always just a 'problem'. And it was the same when the Huguenots came in the seventeenth century. And when the Jews arrived over hundreds of years. We have got to change this national tendency.

Current debates and paranoia

I find British public opinion on migration is too often emotive and uninformed. Just before the European and local elections in May 2014, I was invited by Channel 5 to discuss immigration. They had done one big, blazing debate on benefits that had brought high ratings and I suppose they wanted to repeat this 'success'. So I went on expecting to argue and take on some really lazy thinking. As it happened, I felt increasingly ill at ease; I was discomfited and at times baffled by the hostility. One *Sun* columnist, in particular, was very tough, hard and uncompromising. What was her experience of life? A natural-born, young *Sun* columnist should, I thought, be embracing clever people – white, black, brown, green or whatever colour. Instead, she was attacking their ambition and hard work.

OK, I admit I was like her once – and far more

powerful. I was editor of that paper for twelve years – and yes, we too often maligned immigrants and minorities because we could. They had no redress and many even bought the paper. You get into that world and you never look out.

What I now know is that, as an editor, you don't go and meet people – or *real* people. Editors think they know everything – that they have an umbilical cord to the thought processes of readers – but we don't. I didn't know anybody out there; I barely knew my wife. I just about knew my driver, since I worked such long hours. I definitely didn't know any black or Asian people – I never came across them.

Max Hastings, historian, previous editor and columnist, once wrote that he realised how little contact he had with British Muslims and that he had never had a single Muslim to dinner.[7] That is true, I reckon, for almost all powerful media figures.

Newspapers in general are terrible places for minorities. They are like the police force – white and disconnected.

---

7   'I confess, I have never had a Muslim to dinner', *Sunday Telegraph*, 31 July 2005.

I do remember saying: 'We need to reflect our readers.' I look back now and think how much more could have been done.

We could have developed a positive hiring policy. It made no sense, this wilful exclusion of millions. But I didn't see that then. The business case did not occur to us. Imagine if coffee shops decided to sell only to whites, providing their product for, say, only 72 per cent of the population and systematically excluding a large and increasingly prosperous, high-spending customer base. I didn't think about that at *The Sun*. I was selling 4 million copies and I didn't realise I needed to think beyond that.

Murdoch, for his part, is positive about immigrants. In May 2013, we talked about the rise of UKIP. I advised him that the party would prove to be phenomenally successful.

He asked: 'Are you sure? What should our response be?'

My reply: 'You cannot, and I know you will not, support UKIP. You're in favour of people of all backgrounds getting to the top. If you go down the UKIP route, who knows where it will end?'

He sent back an email saying: 'You are right.'

On that Channel 5 programme I appeared to be the only white person who was prepared to proselytise the pro-minority argument or take on UKIP views. Normally, in most arguments, I do represent the views of millions – or at least I feel I can persuade people to listen to what I have to say. I am used to bear pits, but this was different. Scary, almost. During this programme, no one was listening. Stranger still, when I spoke it went deathly quiet. And then it went quieter and quieter. Usually, when I speak, everyone starts shouting and hollering and I take them on. This time, that didn't happen. I felt more and more like an outsider – uncomfortable. If you are talking into a vacuum, you feel unnerved not strengthened. The wall of silence closed in on me.

I think the programme-makers and those invited on expected me to say I had been really impressed by Nigel Farage and that I was pleased to announce I had been appointed the deputy leader of UKIP. Because I didn't say that, they were wrong-footed. Some must have started to suspect I had taken some funny pills. They must have thought that Kelvin MacKenzie – an old, bald, grey, former editor of *The Sun* – had to be a right-wing toerag. It was prejudice. Prejudgement. It is the kind of prejudice and prejudgement experienced by minorities every day. Racists, in my view, are thick, but here I understood how they must get under the skins of black and Asian people. I felt vaguely threatened and labelled by the crowd. They didn't know my views but they decided they did. I knew then that I had to make this case out there in the public space.

Defending migrants and minorities

Today it seems to me that such a case cannot be made without one being accused of being politically correct or unpatriotic. But a case must be made. That is what I am doing in this short book. First, we need to think about the language we use. The words 'immigrants' and 'migrants' have become pejorative and almost an insult – tainted and muddied. 'Minorities' is neutral and perhaps more useful, though I accept that sometimes we do have to concede words in common usage. And another thing: I know I once was editor of a shouty paper but, being wiser now, I have become aware of how language demeans those who try to come here. Suzanne Moore, herself white and working class, put her finger on it: 'It is becoming acceptable to speak of migrants, refugees and asylum seekers not as human at all but as a kind of infection, an infection that multiplies and then demands school places for its children.' Our nation may decide it doesn't want them, but they are not a disease or rats bringing pestilence. How do they feel – those who are here, working hard and doing their best?

So, to develop my argument further: either we should have completely closed our borders and never invited any workers here in the first place (but we didn't do that) or we should have made sure that those who did come here were valued and not turned on. It's simple. Enterprising Europeans throughout the centuries have gone out into the world to seek better lives. If we understand that, we must surely understand that others around the world have the same dreams and want the same chances. The incomers are participating in our lucky lives – creating wealth for our lucky lives. We like them when they are flogging themselves to death, but when they turn out to have different views on life or vote in a manner that we don't like or follow religions that we don't share then we turn against them.

You look around today and see real evidence of vengeance or anger directed at foreigners that comes across as madness or a syndrome. People's own experiences seem not to affect their fury. If they just totted up how many interactions in a single day are with minorities – and thought about what these incomers do – then they might move beyond the fear, intolerance and envy. Some voices do speak up, and there are many areas of Britain where you don't get this surge of bigotry, but you hardly hear or see them enough in the media. Joe Kelliher, though, a doctor from Newcastle, wrote to *The Guardian*, and is worth quoting at length:

> I came from the west of Ireland to the West End of Newcastle in the early '80s and have practised as a GP ever since. The welcome and generosity of the local people, all exclusively white British, to an Irish man, was greatly appreciated. This was and is a predominantly white, working-class area with high levels of unemployment

and deprivation ... The area was dying. Soon after, immigrants from various parts of the world started to arrive and the demographics of the place have now changed greatly. In my practice, more than 50 per cent of people do not have English as their first language. The West End has been given a new lease of life, with local shops, restaurants and small businesses, private investments, housing and so on. The 'indigenous' people of Newcastle remain open, friendly and kind. The malevolent attempt by racist politicians to shift the blame for the distress caused by government underfunding of social welfare, housing and employment onto the immigrants is shameful.[8]

Now, as most people know, I am on the right, and I think people should help themselves rather than depend on the taxpayer, as they did in this instance. Areas that were going to seed were picked up, livened up, quietly regenerated and made sustainable by the incomers, although one wonders why it took incomers to revitalise the dying area described by this doctor.

---

8   *The Guardian*, Letters to the Editor, 3 June 2014.

We native Britons have our brilliant entrepreneurs too. Just look at the story of Poundland – set up by two guys, Dave Dodd and Stephen Smith, in the middle of the recession. They saw a business opportunity and went for it. Good for them. But it is now forgotten that there already were some £1 shops run by minorities all over inner-city areas – the model was good and was built upon by others. Do we teach our schoolchildren about the contributions of migrants, going back to the Huguenots, Jews and Asians? Why don't we do that? Maybe if we did, people would understand how much our country owes minorities. And some of them would give up the politics of resentment.

Cameron made false promises to get immigration numbers down to 100,000 a year by 2015. He must've known that wouldn't happen. Theresa May rushed even further to the bottom, saying she would reduce the numbers to tens of thousands. The Home Office passes new rulings every day, which are, I think, intended to keep minorities down and out and feeling insecure, while accounting for how important their labour is.

In 2014, *The Spectator* ran an online blog on one of

the new rulings that suggested that to prevent sham marriages, registry offices have to inform the Home Office of marriage and civil partnership bookings and the couples then have to prove they love each other. How do you do that? How do I prove to an official that I love my wife? As the writer Alex Massie said: 'Henceforth British citizens marrying, say, Mexicans or Koreans or Kenyans will have to prove to the state their love is genuine and not a "sham" ... what a dismal, mean-spirited, demeaning state of affairs.' He pointed out that, in the previous twelve months, around 1,300 marriages were found to be fake – not exactly a massive number – but now, all those who offend the state by falling in love with 'bloody foreigners' will be suspect until proven innocent.[9] I thought the Tories were pro-family? We should perhaps worry about what the state is able to do.

I think it is time to point out that no restrictions will be good enough for those who are absolutely against migration and who start panics about it every day. One of the

9   26 November 2014.

most unpleasant of these panics was Migration Watch suggesting we are overrun by 'hidden migrants'. No, not behind false doors in takeaways and underground pipes, but actually out there among us: the children of 'foreign-born' mums. Well, that would be the kids of Nigel Farage then; of Winston Churchill, Nick Clegg, the Milibands … and, if we include foreign-born dads, of the future king of England, his siblings and Boris Johnson. We have the highest rates of mixed-race marriages and relationships in the western world – a real sign of cohesion. Instead of celebrating this, we are warned about the 'impure' children who can never belong in this nation. I don't think Hitler would disagree.

Columnist Matthew d'Ancona, previously deputy editor of the *Sunday Telegraph* and former editor of *The Spectator*, is one of the few voices to take on the UKIP challenge. The clue might lie in his name: his father came from Malta to Britain to study, ended up playing youth football for Newcastle United, stayed on, became a civil servant and married an Englishwoman. The good immigrant story. Their son Matthew was sent to a private school and then Oxford, where he got the top First in modern history for his year (1989). In his piece, d'Ancona dismissed Andrew Green's repeated claim that immigration debates are not permitted in this country:

> Since long before I became properly aware in my teens of proper political argument, there has been vigorous argument in this country about immigration and population mobility ... The figures published by Sir Andrew Green's outfit to demonstrate the supposed effects of 'mass immigration' have frequently been questioned. But Sir Andrew never lost the phoney cool of the ideologue posing as an empiricist ... no pressure group masquerading as a research institute has been so cushily treated by the media, offered pages of space in red-top newspapers or to present its findings on television.[10]

And so the people have turned.

Millions of Brits blame foreigners for traffic jams, for house prices going up, for health services failing.

---

10 'Now Cameron must take the EU battle to UKIP', *Evening Standard*, 22 October 2014.

The truth is that if you keep foreigners out, town centres – including Oxford Street – would die; hospitals and surgeries would not cope; everything we think of as our good life would be good no more. I went to St Andrews, where there is a hotel overlooking the golf course, and realised that if they took eastern Europeans out of St Andrews and this top, five-star hotel, there would be nobody left to keep the place going. These workers come here not knowing much English but, within a very short time, most have picked up the business language of the world. That alone improves their prospects and is our gift to them.

When you start looking into why migrants take to the seas and endure such risks – many even die – you realise that growing markets offer them the only available chance in life. It is that or die. And it isn't an easy option. They are not risking their lives to be on benefits. They want to live, work, survive, make good. Since when did that become a crime? If it *is* now a crime, why do so many enterprising white Europeans go off to live and work in South Africa, Kenya, Canada, the USA and some EU nations? Since the recession, our young graduates are setting off for the Continent to seek their fortunes. Should Germany and France expel and abuse them? And should our Brits who have settled in Spain face ugly public anger because Spain is still in recession? Some research shows that there are more American settlers in the UK than Jamaican immigrants and descendants. We have Australians, New Zealanders, Zimbabweans and South Africans too – do they get accused of taking jobs? I think eastern Europeans are targeted because they are poor and non-EU people are targeted because of their colour.

We know that there are just under a million 16–24-year-olds out of work. The foreigners are not robbing them of jobs. Actually, foreigners are paying their benefits. That is the reality and we should thank the Lord every time we see a foreigner. That is also the message politicians and businesses should be giving out, making policies based on rational grounds not populist agitation.

To carry on with the economic case: in the autumn of 2014, there was a major problem as the apple harvest came along. Too few immigrants had turned up to pick the fruit. One year before this happened, the government had closed the seasonal workers scheme, which had allowed pickers to come in from the EU for a few months and then go back home. In the *Hereford Times*, a representative of the National Union of Farmers complained that he could not hire unemployed British workers because they didn't like the low-paid work and didn't stick at the job. Everyone was losing out.[11] Previously, the EU agricultural pickers earned money, went back and made their lives better; the farmers got their produce; we got our apples when they were fresh. The only people who lost out were Brits who didn't want to put in the back-breaking hours. That, you might say, is a choice. But they then complained and politicians felt they must listen to those who didn't help themselves. Some locals do want the job, but they also want more money for it. That is understandable, although most have

---

11 'More foreign workers needed to do farm work unemployed and "lazy" Brits won't do', *Hereford Times*, 19 September 2014.

made complaining about immigrants their full-time occupation.

Now, I understand most humans will blame foreigners for their troubles. It seems instinctive. But then civilisation is about overcoming some instincts. Here, this blame culture is the only political game in town. Psychologists call it 'projection' and it is irrational. People forget – but I haven't – that it was Margaret Thatcher who wanted a free market in Europe. She may have spoken like a Little Englander – often for political effect – but she encouraged internationalism in business.

A few years back, Evan Davies presented a programme on BBC TV filmed in Wisbech.[12] Employers gave migrant workers time off and got Brits who lived in the town to go and work in fields, factories and businesses. It was a disaster. The locals moaned that they felt like foreigners in their own country, yet most would not get out of bed when given the chance, or found it all too hard. One chap named Lewis still lived with his mum at the age of twenty-six. He had obviously never

---

12 *The Day the Immigrants Left*, BBC One, 24 February 2010.

done an honest job and was not going to. While Polish pickers earned over £150 a day at an asparagus farm, British workers wouldn't pick a handful. Dean, a carpenter, got angry because his factory supervisor was Lithuanian. Sam, an unemployed chef, said, 'I don't like working under pressure.' He was taken on by Ali, who ran the town's busiest Indian restaurant and offered chances to three other unemployed Brits too. Not one of them could stand the heat and pressure. A couple of young people did shape up and prove themselves, but the rest returned to their lazy lives and complaints. It showed us that the English candidates talked big but couldn't deliver.

Instead of hating and humiliating foreign workers and minorities, we should bus white kids from estates to live with those migrants who have strong work ethics. Let them stay there for a month and learn self-discipline, endeavouring and getting wise to the competition out there in the globalised world. They will be lost if they carry on behaving as if everyone owes them something. Power is moving east and this is when we need our countries to be strong and efficient.

The difficulties and drawbacks

There is no such thing as a free lunch. Immigration brings advantages as well as problems. We are a small island and we do have to control numbers. A small country has to have limits on population growth, otherwise it is not sustainable. I don't think newcomers should get benefits and free health service for the first six months, except in real emergencies. There is pressure on our resources. Asians, black people and eastern Europeans aren't all angels (but they aren't born devils either). The reality is that there's good and bad in everyone. It's nothing to do with race. Among whites there are incidents of terrible cruelty or criminal activity – sometimes the people involved will be lawyers, doctors or businessmen. We don't racialise the crime. We don't expect people to say all white men are paedophiles because Jimmy Savile and Cyril Smith abused boys.

The far more serious problem is that some cultural groups have indefensible attitudes and behaviours. How they treat women, for example, or how certain mainly Pakistani grooming gangs in towns and cities systematically corrupt and abuse young, white girls. And then we have the Islamicists. They are a real threat to our way of life. Many of them were born and raised here but we need to be tough with them. The deal is non-negotiable: you live and work here and make a better future for your families; in return, this nation expects you to be law-abiding, to learn English and to live by its rules. Social services, local authorities, the police and educators must have a zero-tolerance policy on child marriages, honour beatings or killings, the ensnarement of white girls, forced marriages and plots against the state. We have laws for that and they must be enforced regardless of ethnic sensitivities. We should not separate children into single-faith schools. We now see segregation for the first time in our history and that cannot be allowed to happen.

Integration policies are central. All communities, including the English, Scottish, Welsh and Irish, have a duty to integrate with those unlike themselves, to buy into diversity and unity. Minorities have the same duties and responsibilities. I have heard that some Asians don't want their children to have white friends. That is also racism. And it is wrong.

The good news

But, again, we must remember how far we have come. We have a man of Pakistani heritage, Sajid Javid, as the Culture, Media and Sports Minister. Labour has the smooth-talking Chuka Umunna – again, a man with real leadership qualities. Mishal Husain presents BBC Radio 4's *Today* programme. Mo Farah was a refugee to whom we gave a home. Look how he has paid us back. His twin back home never got that chance.

That is what we need to be proud about: when something in our culture meets immigrant cultures and great things are born. It is a bit like the children of mixed relationships – they can often be brighter and more handsome than the sum of their parts. Instead of longing to bring back the days of *Downton Abbey*, we need to celebrate what we have achieved by not being closed-off.

I sent a young student down to Oxford to talk to residents – insiders and outsiders; students and lecturers; shoppers and managers. This ancient city is famously full of toffs, but that is not all it is. It once had one of the biggest car-making plants in the world – still there, but much smaller now – and there have long been tensions between the students and the civvies, although this has changed in the last twenty years. The population has surged, there is too much traffic, not enough housing and a continuing division between privileged students, although colleges are now taking in working-class and minority children like never before and unemployment rates are lower than average. I wanted to find out what young people feel about this dynamic, multicultural city, where previously time stood still for centuries.

The researcher, herself of Bangladeshi origins, talked to around thirty people on the streets, outside colleges, at taxi ranks, in shops and elsewhere. None of them expressed hostility towards foreigners or migrants. Six did say they were angry about grooming gangs in Oxford, around ten were worried about Indian and Chinese students getting the best jobs, and the children of car workers were anxious because the car company was cutting jobs. But the informal research showed that our young people can be very open-minded and easy towards diversity. The hope is that, as they get older, they won't lose that ease or turn inwards. Or vote UKIP.

I think they might, though, unless we change the conversations about migrants and minorities.

The next section provides the hard facts and figures, as well as the cultural contributions of minorities. Those who oppose migration have their own figures but, in the end (and in my view), the anti-immigrant case is weak and unsustainable. What have the immigrants ever done for us? Everything.[13]

---

13 *The Day the Immigrants Left*, BBC One, 24 February 2010.

Part II

Part II

Lies, truths, prejudices
and statistics

REMEMBER THE THREE wise monkeys who saw, heard and spoke no evil? You used to see them on mantelpieces – wooden or ceramic chimps with paws over their eyes, ears and mouths. I suppose they told people not to gossip or leer – and to mind their own business. We should bring the monkeys back, but this time as a warning. Look, listen, speak up – before it is too late.

Millions of Britons have become so anti-immigrant they seem to be blind and deaf to the facts and evidence right there in front of their noses. If you give them economic reasons to be positive, they bring up culture; if you make cultural and historical arguments, they start talking about benefit scroungers and austerity. Somehow we have got to get them out of this mentality. Would they prefer it if farmers left apples to rot, buses were taken out of service and hospitals could not function, just to keep out the 'bloody foreigners'?

Politicians of all parties are too cowardly. They follow the herd, encourage prejudices, try to appease the 'old, pessimistic, male voters frightened – not unreasonably – at a time of change amid economic storms'.[14] By this I mean people like Gerald Howarth, a Tory MP who complained that Nepalese settlers were taking up park benches in Aldershot. These settlers are Gurkhas and their families – men who have been an elite fighting force in the British Army for decades. How did it get this bad?[15]

The media, too, often reinforces prejudices. Imagine how it would unnerve UKIP if *The Sun* or the *Mail* regularly published big, bold features on what immigrants have given this country. The world view and self-pity of

---

14 Ian Birrell, *The Observer*, 9 May 2013.

15 See press reports on 26 March 2012.

those readers – many of whom are possibly UKIP voters – would crumble. And a very good thing that would be, too. Broadcasters seem to have lost their heads over this party. Farage appears over a dozen times on *Question Time* – free advertisement for him at our expense. Who else has had such easy access to our public service broadcaster? Not me, that's for sure.

We have to get real. A report by the Institute for Public Policy Research concluded:

> The UK is now one of the most diverse countries in the developed world ... The current coalition has tried (but failed) to substantially bring down overall immigration ... It is more or less inevitable that the UK will continue to be a country of high immigration for the foreseeable future.[16]

After all these years of banging the 'keep out' drum, what do we find? In November 2014, the independent

---

16 'Shared Ground', Alice Sachrajda & Phoebe Griffiths, Institute for Public Policy Research, 2014, p.3.

head of the immigration inspectorate alleged that his reports were being interfered with and politicised. And that, in my view, is because the coalition government is in a flap; terrified since they have not been able to cut numbers. So, of course, UKIP then jump up and down – well, they would, wouldn't they? The numbers can't go down because we are in the EU and because we are not yet 'fortress Britain'. Maybe, as the comedian Mark Steel suggested, Mrs May should have the Channel Tunnel filled with piranhas.[17]

It isn't just the right that has turned anti-immigrant, though. We have some self-important gurus on the left, too – David Goodhart, for example. For ten years he has banged on about how diversity makes the nation more divided and less together, speaking of the natural need for us to be with 'our own sort'. He even argues that the welfare state can only be maintained if most of us are the same race and ethnicity.[18] Well, I say to him: try running the welfare state without migrants, both past

---

17 *The Independent*, 3 October 2013.

18 See his book *The British Dream*, Atlantic Books, 2013.

and present. Even the *Telegraph*'s reviewer slammed him.[19] Does Goodhart know or care that 26 per cent of NHS doctors are of Indian origin? Does he count the nurses, reception staff, wheelchair pushers and volunteers in hospitals who come from elsewhere? Does he notice the faces of men of every colour in sharp suits in the City?

What we need to do is learn how to manage integration, ensure fairness, bring people together, deal with segregation – white or black – and prevent hostilities in an age of high migration, greater diversity and increased mobility.[20]

You can of course be pro- or anti-European, for or against immigration – but not just because you feel like it. Facts matter. Here is some of the solid, independent, creditable evidence missing in action. Don't cover your eyes and ears. If, once you have read and absorbed it, you still keep fast to your negative views, then you will prove that rationality cannot always break down the

---

19 Review by Ian Thompson, 9 April 2013.

20 The IPPR report I refer to above suggests policies for better integration.

walls of strongly held beliefs. Trust me. If I can change my views, anyone can.

Our immigration policies do not serve our nation well. When we go through hard times, public anxieties rise and immigrants are inevitably blamed. Governments become hostages to the national mood instead of doing what's best for Britain. As an Indian journalist wrote recently: 'The triumph of politics over pragmatism tends to be most assured when the economy is faltering, because it is precisely when people are feeling economically vulnerable that the immigration debate becomes most toxic.'[21]

Just when good politicians should be giving out accurate information, they roll over. And so the exaggerations and misinformation build up. Take the UKIP victories in the local elections of May 2014. Everyone was swept away by the 'earthquake', as the media put it. Well, their national vote share actually fell. It was 17 per cent, compared with 23 per cent in the local elections a year earlier. There are no UKIP-controlled

---

21   Sonia Sodha, *The Observer*, 24 February 2013.

councils and only 163 seats out of 4,211 council seats went to the party.[22] You see, numbers count and can chase out myths.

History

We need to remember history. In 1972, Great Britain was a basket case economically and Enoch Powell was the most popular politician around – much more powerful and imposing than Nigel Farage. Suddenly, that August, came news of the mass expulsion of Asians from Uganda, most of whom had British nationality. Racism shot up, people and the popular press were alarmed, hysterical even. The mood was as ugly as it is today. Leicester and Ealing councils put full-page adverts in Ugandan newspapers asking the Asians not to move into their areas because they were 'full up'. But *The Economist* wrote this:

> Welcome, British passport holders. We know many of
> you really didn't want to leave your homes and jobs in

---

22 See the independent information service www.bellenden.co.uk.

Uganda. You know we didn't really want you to come before because we have problems with homes and jobs here. But most of us believe that this is a country that can use your skills and energies. We have worked out plans about how you should start and where you should go. They won't be perfect but they will help. You will find that we, like other countries, have our bullies and misfits. We are particularly sorry about those of our politicians who are trying to use your troubles for their own ends. And we are glad the British passport means something again.[23]

The Economist – still avidly pro-immigration – was right. In the East Midlands these escapees from Idi Amin have created more than 30,000 jobs.[24] Their children are rising in many professions – law, medicine, accountancy, pharmacy, investment banking, politics and others. Ask our supermarkets and service stations, they will tell you that 'foreign' workers have a strong

---

23   19 August 1972.

24   BBC News, 8 November 2002.

work ethic that rubs off on white Britons – if and when they work together.[25]

The thing is we turned on every group that came into the country in high numbers. We were hostile to Huguenots, Jews, Caribbeans, Ugandan Asians, Pakistanis, Indians, the Chinese and the Vietnamese. The country is always full up. Huguenots set up the Bank of England; Caribbeans gave their lives to the NHS and our transport services; Ugandan Asians started 24-hour shopping; Jews gave us books, art and retail mega-businesses.

But we don't thank them; we just pick on the next lot.

The EU and non-EU numbers and policies

One of the most disturbing facts is that the British public significantly overestimates the numbers of minorities and migrants in this country. When asked

---

25 See 'What are the impacts of economic migration to the UK?', Rachel Maran-gozov, Institute for Employment Studies, Issue 8, July 2008.

by Ipsos MORI researchers what percentage of the nation's population is foreign-born, the figure the public came up with was 31 per cent. The real figure is 13 per cent. The public also believed that 21 per cent of Britons are Muslim, when Muslims in fact make up only 5 per cent of the population.[26] The public needs to be better educated on this emotive subject.

There are, at present, over six million working adults in the UK who were born abroad. The proportion has doubled since 1995 and did not, unusually, fall during the last recession. EU migrants account for 28 per cent of the total figure of migrants.[27]

But let us compare the UK to other European nations. As we've said, the percentage of British citizens born abroad is 13 per cent. Compare this with France and Germany (12 per cent), Spain (14 per cent), Ireland (16 per cent) and Switzerland (29 per cent).[28] And, by the

---

26 International Study published on 29 October 2014.

27 'Immigration, the European Union and the UK Labour Market', Jonathan Wadsworth et al., Centre for Economic Performance (CEP), Paper 015, May 2014.

28 UCL, Centre for Research and Analysis of Migration factsheet.

way, 7.5 per cent of native Britons live abroad. So much for us having the highest migrant population.

In a referendum in December 2014, Switzerland, one of the most conservative European nations, rejected by 74 per cent to 26 per cent a proposal to severely curtail immigration.[29] When the moment of reckoning came, the Swiss realised just what immigrants gave to their country.

The Institute for Public Policy Research has asserted that not only do we need migrants to maintain economic growth and stability, but we need them to stick around so their contributions are sustained. Some areas don't reap the benefits of migration because the incomers are short-time workers who come and go. Migrants expand markets, add to the skills pool and enliven areas.[30]

Now, it is true that some wages can be pushed down, but not nearly as much as is claimed and not forever. What's more, government studies suggest that

---

29 This was on 1 December. See report in *The Economist*, 2 December 2014.

30 See report by Laura Chappell, IPPR, April 2008.

these incomers have had no adverse impact on the wages or employment prospects of local workers.[31] Yet, somehow, one House of Lords committee report concluded that immigration had low or no impact on the economic well-being of Britons and that foreigners were an obstacle to the training and pay of young UK workers.[32] Sorry, m'Lords. That is just bunkum. Plenty of other solid, independent evidence says the opposite.

According to a report from the Centre for Economic Planning (CEP) at the London School of Economics, there can be economic benefits to migration and there is little evidence of an overall negative impact on employment or wages for native workers, except for some in low-skilled jobs.[33]

Europeans who moved to the UK for work after 2000 have paid more in taxes than they have received

---

31 See 'The impact of migration from the new European Union member states on native workers', S. Lemos & J. Portes, 2008, commissioned by the Department for Work and Pensions.

32 'The Economic Impact of Immigration', April 2008.

33 Wadsworth, op. cit.

in benefits, helping to lighten the tax burdens on UK-born workers as this money has contributed to public service finances. Between 2000 and 2011, they added £20 billion to the state coffers and they have provided human capital to the UK that would have otherwise cost us £6.8 billion in education and training. These are research findings from a report published in 2014 by University College, London.[34] And what did Iain Duncan Smith say about this report, written by two internationally respected professors? That the findings were 'silly'. You know what that means: he doesn't want to know the facts because they are inconvenient.

People forget too that 7.5 per cent of UK citizens currently live abroad, so let me say it again. Most left this country for the same reasons people come into it: to better themselves and, in time, to contribute to the land of settlement. In 2006, for example, 400,000 Brits went to live in Australia, New Zealand, Spain or France. Why is that not a problem?

---

34 'Positive economic impact of UK immigration from the European Union', Professor Christian Dustmann & Dr Tommaso Frattini, November 2014.

What will happen if we leave the EU?

Almost half of all UK exports go to the EU. That is almost 15 per cent of the GDP. One cost of leaving the EU – 'Brexit' – would be less trade, according to the CEP. Using economic models, the forecasts predict income losses of around 3.1 per cent (£50 billion) in the pessimistic case or 1.1 per cent (£18 billion) in the optimistic case. There would also be 'further effects on immigration, foreign investment and regulations. Although harder to quantify, Brexit is also likely to, on balance, depress income through these channels.'

More real information as opposed to wild claims then. Between 2004 and 2009, 1.5 million eastern Europeans came to the UK. During that period, Britain's GDP grew by £98 billion.[35] Are we really going to take no notice of this phenomenal growth that helped cushion us from the worst effects of the last recession?

At the CBI conference in the autumn of 2014, John Cridland, the collective's director general, said:

---

35 'Eastern European migrants "add £5bn" to Britain's GDP', BBC News, May 2011.

EU migration is essential for a healthy economy. I understand that cultural and social impacts can't be ignored but, as head of one of the UK's biggest business groups, I am concerned about where the debate on immigration is heading. I know other business leaders share this unease. There is a mismatch between rhetoric and reality. Immigration has helped keep the wheels of this recovery turning by plugging skills shortages. This has led to more jobs for British people and driven growth. Recovery would grind to a halt without the free movement of people.

Cridland comes from Boston in Lincolnshire, where a large number of eastern Europeans moved to in order to do seasonal work and set up small businesses. To him, this is not a loss but a gain – newcomers have added vibrancy to a place that had perhaps become static. He is not only concerned about profits, though. He recognises that: 'Our care homes and hospitals would not function without overseas workers. Building sites that we need in order to deliver more homes and infrastructure projects would also stall.'[36]

---

36 *Daily Telegraph*, 25 October 2014.

I believe strongly that if Britain exits from the EU it needs to do so for real, good and considered reasons. And, be honest, it would still not end migration. We cannot close or police our borders totally. Such a total cut-off from the world is unachievable. Everyone in power knows that, but they all play the game and pretend they can in order to keep the masses quiet. Yet the people no longer keep quiet, because they too know it can't be done. This 'zero migration' is just a fantasy.

And one more thing: the Office for National Statistics confirms that two-thirds of EU migrants come here to work, not to get benefits. A fifth come to study. Those who lead this country – and I mean those from every party – are no longer thinking straight about migration and minorities. They are letting themselves get carried away by the winds of protest and so the policies they come up with are not only poorly thought through, but many are also, in my view, completely nutty.

Here are some examples…

Bad policy

- New policies are making it harder for overseas students to attend universities just when our universities need good students from abroad in a competitive market.

- The government is making it much harder for family members to settle in this country. This and the 'control' above means that global talent is choosing not to come to Britain. The pool of international talent has been reduced.[37]

- It is not sustainable for the government to impose bureaucratic hurdles while claiming to have an open door for 'desirable' incomers. It doesn't make sense. Many key institutions have reservations about the system favoured by politicians where a migrant must have a job and skills needed by particular employers.[38]

---

37 'Highly skilled migration to the UK, 2007–2013', Migration Observatory, 2014.

38 See 'Attracting Skilled Immigrants: An Overview of Recent Policy Developments in Advanced Countries', G. Facchini & E. Lodigiani, NIESR, 2014.

The whole business is cumbersome and could lead to crises in some sectors – Indian restaurants, for example.

- An employer-driven system of admission is much less effective than migrant-driven schemes. It is also fairer. Canada has made migrant-driven schemes the mainstay of their skill-selective immigration policy.

- The pool of international talents who have higher education and occupational experience or qualifications is getting smaller.

- Skills shortages reduce productivity and lead to delayed contracts and delivery.[39]

One reason for the lack of evidence-based, rational immigration policies in the UK is public opinion. With the election looming no party is prepared to make the case for migration. As British Influence points out,

---

39 Ibid.

what has been lacking is real leadership. Public opinion cannot become an alternative government.

The economy and the private and public sectors

So now we know. Migrant labour is more productive, cost-effective and good for economic drive in a number of ways. Then there is what they spend, of course. Ask any retailer how their customer base has expanded since these arrivals and they will tell you. Go to TK Maxx and see how many of their workers and customers are 'foreign'.

Do you know anyone who hasn't employed Polish builders, workmen or gardeners? I don't. OK, so then the class issue is raised – and justifiably, in my view. It is the middle classes who have benefited from the recent migrant labour. But why is that? I know of people who wanted to employ 'true Brit' house cleaners and were willing to pay above the minimum wage. They tried but they got no takers. In some of the smaller towns outside big cities, local people are actually prepared to take up cleaning and manual jobs, but the numbers are small and geographically restricted. One thing is indisputable: Britons living in areas of high unemployment would not 'migrate' to places where they could get low-paid jobs. But that is what migrants do. Graduate Poles will do the painting and decorating, saving up until they can make something of their lives. It is what Asians did, too. I don't blame the Brits who don't want to work hard for not much money. It is a choice. But I do blame them for blaming others who do. Not a single industry in our country can say it is 'pure' British and proud.

We already have signs of reverse migration – 8 per cent of Poles have now left the country.[40] The recession and the national mood are responsible. I talk to business people and they are worried, not only about workers leaving, but about a fall in consumer base.

Here is yet more evidence showing how much immigrants do for themselves and us...

40 *The Times*, 18 February 2008.

The GDP

- A study quoted by the Office for Budget Responsibility (OBR) found that migrant labour had a small positive effect (0.17 per cent) on the UK's economic growth between 1987 to 2005.[41]

- A study of OECD countries found that greater immigration led to greater growth through increased employment.[42]

- The OBR calculates a reduction in growth if immigration is lower than it has been.

- As migrants are mostly of working age, they are less of a burden than those in the general population, which has an increasing number of people aged over sixty.

---

41 Fiscal sustainability report, 2013.

42 'A Global View of Cross-Border Migration', F. Ortega & G. Peri, Social Science Research Network, 2009.

- Between 2004 and 2009, eastern Europeans added £5 billion to the GDP.[43]

- A predictive modelling study based on policy intentions to substantially reduce immigration to the UK concluded that, if this policy were to happen, GDP would fall by 11 per cent by 2060 and the drop would be felt by everybody.[44]

- New figures show that immigrants who have arrived here since 2000 have contributed more than £20 billion to the public purse.

- Between 2001 and 2011, EU migrants from the EU15 countries gave 64 per cent more than they got back in benefits. Those who joined later gave 12 per cent more than they received.[45]

---

43 BBC News, May 2011.

44 'The Long-Term Economic Impact of Reducing Migration in the UK', K. Lisenkova, M. Mérette & M. Sanchez-Martinez, NIESR, 2013.

45 'The Fiscal Effects of Migration to the UK', Professor Christian Dustmann & Dr Tommaso Frattini, *Economic Journal*, 5 November 2014.

- There is some evidence that migrants are relatively more likely to be innovative and that diverse workforces bring new perspectives, experiences and knowledge.[46]

- The ONS has found that although only 1 per cent of the UK's registered businesses are foreign-owned, they contributed 28 per cent of the UK's approximate value added tax.[47]

Productivity, wages, innovation and employment[48]

- Skilled migrants improve the productivity of others, according to the Oxford Migration Observatory.

---

46 'Does Cultural Diversity Help Innovation in Cities: Evidence from London Firms', SERC discussion paper, M. Nathan, Spatial Economics Research Centre, LSE, 2011.

47 'Business Ownership in the UK, 2011', 24 October 2013.

48 The list below comes from various papers and reports produced by the Migration Observatory. For example, 'Responding to Employers: Labour Shortage and Immigration Policy' by M. Ruhs and B. Anderson, 2011. Also useful is data from the National Institute for Economic and Social Research and the Centre for Economic Performance.

Migrant skills complement those of skilled British workers and this raises collective output.

- Increases in earnings would be felt by median earners, but lower earners would get less out of them. (This is a serious problem that governments need to tackle independently of the migration question. A living wage for all should be the basis of our society.)

- There is little evidence of immigration having a negative impact on jobs or wages in the UK, according to the Centre for Economic Performance.

- The CEP also found that youth unemployment in the UK rose less in areas of high immigration and greater diversity. This is not what we ever hear on our broadcast channels or from the mouths of politicians.

- Diversity encourages and improves innovation. This happens because migrants and minorities bring new perspectives, experiences and knowledge.

- According to a team of Oxford researchers, countries with mixed populations benefit from the 'diversity dividend'. Local and national economies become more dynamic and less stale or staid.

- Migrants often start up small businesses or choose self-employment. They do this to escape a hostile labour market and survive hard times. Pakistanis, Indians, Bangladeshis, Turks and now Poles all take this route.

- Migrant businesses create jobs and opportunities in local areas and the businesses can create a social hub, break barriers and decrease separation.

- Migrants are key to widening international markets – they open doors in their home nations, have an intimate knowledge of the language and culture and can facilitate trade.

- Almost a third of the businesses surveyed by the London Chamber of Commerce employed non-EU workers in order to benefit from their language skills.[49]

- There are notable instances of migrant businesses succeeding in spite of difficult circumstances and this is partly because they go beyond established sectors.[50]

- Access to foreign talent boosts export potential. Migrants bring an intimate knowledge of the language and culture of a trading partner.[51]

- Businesses agree that local people should be up-skilled and they are willing to support this. But that long-term aim does not meet short-term needs.

---

49 'Migration Reform', O. Segade & V. O'Keefe, London Chamber of Commerce, 2011.

50 'The Contribution of New Migrant Entrepreneurs in the UK', T. Jones, M. Ram, Y. Li & P. Edwards, Centre for Entrepreneurs, 2014.

51 'The Business Case for Immigration Reform', T. Papworth, London: Centre Forum, 2013.

In December 2013, the director (himself a migrant) of
the Institute of Directors, the Adam Smith Institute
and the Institute of Economic Affairs wrote a letter to
a newspaper:

> The government's new migration cap is hurting Brit-
> ain's economic recovery and long-term fiscal health
> … Entrepreneurship is being affected too: more than
> a quarter of Silicon Roundabout start-up founders are
> foreign-born and more than half of tech start-ups in
> California's Silicon Valley are immigrants. The cap on
> immigrants is a cap on the innovative industries Brit-
> ain needs to thrive. According to the Office of Budget
> Responsibility, without net migration of at least 260,000
> people per annum, the public debt will approach
> 100 per cent of GDP. The cap does not discriminate
> between the small number of welfare tourists and the
> many people who would like to work productively to
> create a better life for themselves and their families.

Families, yes, and – I would add – their adopted nation.
A recent report refuted claims that foreign workers

are depriving true-born British workers of jobs, which is the central political argument in our country at present. Youth unemployment started rising prior to 2004, before Poles and other eastern Europeans began arriving in high numbers.

Jonathan Portes, the director of the National Institute of Economical and Social Research and former chief economist at the Cabinet Office, took on Migration Watch, the influential anti-immigrant lobby group, saying:

> [Migration Watch] published a report highlighting the 'remarkable coincidence between the rise of youth unemployment and the huge surge in immigration from eastern Europe over the last eight years'. But most published studies suggest immigration has little impact on employment and unemployment. As far as we can tell … unemployment didn't rise faster (or fall more slowly) in areas where migration was higher.[52]

---

52 *The Independent*, 10 January 2012.

Public services and employment[53]

- EU migrants are less likely to work in the public sector than the private sector. Some 26 per cent of UK-born people work in public services, compared with 21 per cent of migrants. Of non-EU migrants, 23 per cent are employed in the public sector. In fact, non-EU migrants make a disproportionately large contribution to the provision of public services in some UK regions. The health service particularly benefits from their skills.

- Some 64 per cent of all non-EU public sector workers are employed in skilled professions within the public sector. Only 52 per cent of native-born Britons fall into this professional and managerial category.

- Foreign-born workers are increasingly employed in the care of older people. In 2008, 35 per cent of nurses looking after the elderly and frail were migrants.

---

53 I have used the Migration Advisory Committee analysis for this section and the research carried out by Dustmann & Frattini, op.cit.

- On average, non-EU migrants employed in the public sector are younger and better educated than UK-born public sector workers.[54]

Education and skills

We are so far gone that we don't even heed the voices of some of the wisest men in this country. The new vice-chancellor of Cambridge University is the son of Polish émigrés. Leszek Borysiewicz knew just one English phrase when he arrived here with his parents: 'Please can I go to the toilet?' His teachers were dedicated to him, gave him extra lessons and took him for walks where they would point out and name grass, trees, streams...

He says bilingualism was a great advantage for education. In Britain we have a tendency to hate other languages. Borysiewicz thinks this is completely wrong because speaking another language gives a child additional opportunities. He adds: 'One of Britain's greatest

54 See 'Analysis of the impacts of migration', Migration Advisory Committee, and 'The impact of migration on the provision of UK public services', C. Dustmann & T. Frattini, 2011.

strengths has been the way it has assimilated so many different communities and we are a very plural and open society.'[55]

Not any more.

The impact of immigration on schools is disproportionately large. Some 15 per cent of the education budget is spent on the children of immigrants when they compose 13 per cent of the population. However, in October 2014, when UKIP was becoming increasingly popular, a study actually found that the key to successful schools is having lots of pupils from different ethnic minorities.[56]

Analysis by the University of Bristol shows that London's schools have benefited from having more migrants coming into the city. It is argued that ethnic minority pupils have greater ambition and aspirations and work harder at school. An even more positive picture emerges in Birmingham, where schools outperform the rest of England. Birmingham has one of the

---

55 *The Guardian*, 3 June 2014.

56 'Impact of migration on the consumption of education and children's services and the consumption of health services, social care and social services', A. George, H. Metcalfe & H. Rolfe, NIESR, 2011.

most mixed populations in Britain and the outperforming ethnic minority pupils are from both disadvantaged neighbourhoods as well as wealthier suburbs.

According to Ofsted, London has the highest proportion of minority children in its schools and the capital's secondary schools have performed better and improved faster since 2003 than anywhere else in the country.

Overall, children from migrant and minority groups do better than white children from similar backgrounds. A pro-learning culture and resistance to 'laddish' youth culture is one key factor.[57]

Children most likely to gain five A* –C grades (above the white British mean) are those from Chinese, Sri Lankan Tamil, Iranian, east African Asian, Vietnamese, Indian, Nigerian, Ghanaian, Bangladeshi and Sierra Leonean backgrounds.

Sir Michael Wilshaw, the chief inspector of schools, said in June 2014:

---

57 See, for example, 'British Chinese Pupils and Parents' Construction of the Value of Education', Becky Francis, Roehampton University, 2005.

White, low-income families' children do the worst of all
in the system. They need attention, but instead of blaming
migrants, we should know that they are raising standards
and our place in international league tables. Immigrant
families are adding value to this nation's performance.
It is not about poverty, but family belief in education.

Now, miserablists will say that migrants are getting all the
resources and attention and that poor white kids are being
neglected. If they can get out of that mindset then they
can actually use the same strategies to get their children
to achieve too. But it is easier to complain about them.

Higher education and skilled adults

In 2012 and 2013, the number of overseas students
dropped for the first time in twenty-nine years.[58] Most
universities, however, need the income and presence
of these students both for economic and reputational
reasons.

---

58 *DailyTelegraph*, 2 April 2014.

In October 2014, the vice-chancellor of Oxford University attacked Britain's immigration policies, which deter foreign students from coming to this country. Andrew Hamilton called it 'vainglorious point-scoring':

> Wherever I travel in the world, particularly in China and India, one question persists: why has the UK adopted a visa system so hostile to student entry? I do my best to answer but, frankly, my question baffles me as well ... why are we doing this to them – and to ourselves?

John O'Keefe, a Nobel prize-winner, also feels that immigration rules are a 'very, very large obstacle' to recruiting the best scientists in the world.[59]

• A fifth of businesses need skilled people they cannot currently find in the British labour pool. They accept that local people need to be trained, but here and now they need to find the best talent available.

---

59 *The Times*, 8 October 2014.

- Immigrants from the EU and beyond account for 20 per cent of professionals in strategically important areas such as oil and gas extraction and aerospace, computer, electronic and optical engineering.

- Good employers want to find good graduates, provide in-house training and encourage school leavers, but they also want to be able to employ migrants with skills not easily found thus far.

- Skilled migrants are more likely than skilled resident workers to specialise in jobs requiring analytical and quantitative skills. Migrants of this kind were not substitutes for UK resident workers but enabled organisations to build teams of experts with complementary skills.[60]

- Such cooperation between nations boosts economic activity in both countries and helps creates jobs. Even

---

60 P. Luccino et al., NIESR discussion paper 386.

if the current skills shortage in Britain were filled by re-skilled British workers, companies would still see many benefits in bringing in some immigrants to work because of the value they add.[61]

Welfare

- There is now reliable data to show that the impact of migration on welfare spending is minimal. The Labour Force Survey has collated figures and can demonstrate that non-UK nationals are less likely to use the benefits system than British nationals. However, Asian and African men, and European men from outside the EU, were higher-than-average claimants among migrants.[62]

- There is also no persuasive evidence that the UK's benefits system acts as a magnet for new migrants.

---

61 'Skilled Immigration and Strategically Important Skills in the Economy', A. George, L. Mumtaz et al., NIESR, 2012.

62 Much of this information comes from, 'A Fair Deal on Migration', IPPR, 2014.

- Some thinkers and campaigners claim that immigration erodes cohesion and could end the welfare state. A study of twenty-one OECD countries over thirty years showed no evidence that countries with a large immigrant population were unable to maintain their welfare state.

- Reports claim £2 billion is spent on health tourism – that is, on people who come over to get free health treatment. This figure is misleading. It includes foreign-born people who pay tax, as well as students, visitors and seasonal workers. Those who come deliberately to access free healthcare cost the country £60–80 million a year, 0.06 per cent of the NHS budget.[63]

- In 2008, migrants composed 19 per cent of carers and 35 per cent of nursing roles in older care. The number of foreign care workers has been increasing faster than immigration in general.[64]

---

63 See 'Quantitative Assessment of Visitor and Migrant Use of the NHS in England', Prederi, Department of Health, 2013.

64 'Migrant Care Workers in Ageing Societies', A. Cangiano et al., Centre on Migration, Policy and Society, 2009.

- On the whole, recent immigrants claim less in benefits than indigenous Brits. These migrant households pay more in taxes than is spent on them. There is no, or very limited, evidence that immigration is driven by welfare generosity. It is the labour market that attracts them.

- Immigrants use the health services as much as native-born Britons, but most are typically healthier because they are young and fit. Remember, though, that one in five health professionals is an immigrant.

- Not all immigrants are entitled to benefits. In fact, immigrants who arrived here since 2000 are 43 per cent less likely to receive benefits or tax credits than native Britons.[65]

- Expenditure on healthcare for migrants is 20 per cent lower than for native Britons.

---

65 Dustmann & Frattini, op.cit.

Diversity, integration, cohesion and well-being

Here is another set of facts people might be surprised to know: white people who live in ethnically diverse areas become less racially prejudiced as time goes by; those who live in monocultural or segregated areas don't become less racist. 'Even if white people have little inter-action with other groups living in the same ethnically diverse community, they feel more tolerant purely because they witness positive interactions between dif-ferent racial groups.' It is called 'passive tolerance' and it helps with social ease, health and well-being.[66]

There are millions of people, and experts too, who have come to believe strongly that difference is a prob-lem, that it makes social cohesion harder and that it lowers social capital. In small parts of the UK, this is cer-tainly the case. However, as Danny Dorling, geographer and professor, has shown in his work over many years,

---

66 An international comparative study was carried out by Professor Miles Hewstone of Oxford University with others. Reported in *The Independent*, 4 March 2014.

class divisions are the real barriers to social cohesion. In a very useful think piece he states categorically that, although racism is rife, we are not sleepwalking into segregation by ethnic grouping: 'Britain does not have racial ghettos in the US sense. Data from the latest Census shows that segregation is decreasing, racial integration improving. Widespread white flight is just a myth. The great divide now is social, income-determined.'[67]

But Manchester University research goes even further. The problem is deprivation, not diversity, according to Professor James Nazroo: 'Our research is all about setting the record straight on those diverse neighbourhoods that are so widely stigmatised. So often we read in our newspapers and hear from our politicians that immigration and ethnic diversity adversely affect a neighbourhood. But careful research shows this to be wrong.'[68]

---

67 *The Guardian*, 24 September 2005.

68 'Diversity is good for your health', University of Manchester, 31 May 2009. See also 'Sleepwalking To Segregation? Challenging Myths about Race and Migration', Nissa Finney & Ludi Simpson, Policy Press, 2009.

Culture, idols and winners

Remember the Olympics? Do we? Just think about those heady days and other obvious examples. Or maybe they are not obvious to people who don't want to know.

There would be no cheap EasyJet if Sir Stelios Haji-Ioannou hadn't come up with a win–win model. The low-cost travel so many working-class people enjoy is thanks to him – a Greek-Cypriot immigrant. M&S, our very British company, was co-founded by Michael Marks – from Belarus. Tesco came out of the striving, determined Jack Cohen – son of a Polish Jewish migrant. Cobra beer is made by an Indian – Karan Bilimoria. He sits in the Lords.[69]

In politics we have Boris Johnson (who has some Turkish heritage), Chuka Umunna, Sayeeda Warsi and Sajid Javid, as well as Anita Rani, who is a superb broadcaster.

Look at the actors – Idris Elba, Meera Syal, Sanjeev Bhaskar, Lenny Henry – and the writers – Andrea Levy,

---

69 See 'Immigration a Bad Thing? 10 Iconic Businesses Founded by People Born Abroad', Huffington Post, 9 May 2013.

Zadie Smith, Salman Rushdie, Gurinder Chadha (who made that terrific film *Bend It Like Beckham*). I mean, how much has Britain gained from them? Sports would collapse without migrants and the children of minorities. English cricket and football would die.

Food is the most striking and obvious example of the cultural riches that are brought by peoples of the world to these isles. Every week, 2.5 million customers eat at curry restaurants. The business is worth £3.6 billion.[70] New immigration restrictions are making it harder to get south Asian chefs. Schools are opening up but the skills shortage is creating a crisis in one of the most vibrant sectors. In August 2013, celebrity chef Jamie Oliver said that all his restaurants would close without European workers: there just aren't the British workers to take their place.

Blame, prejudice and public attitudes

Having an immigrant background doesn't necessarily make someone pro-immigrant. Michael Portillo, Peter

---

70 See statistics produced by the Curry Club.

Hain and Simon Danczuk have been anything but. Oh, and Jeremy Hunt, whose wife is Chinese, says he wants to reduce immigration in order to protect his mixed-race children – a fairly incomprehensible position. Mixed marriage and fatherhood have clearly not made him open to others, so I guess you never can tell. The powerful in our country know the facts about the economic and social benefits of migration but they allow people to carry on resenting the outsiders.

Political cowardice and leadership failures have led to a crisis. Facts and truths count for nothing and people seem programmed to hate migrants and minorities. Attitudes towards immigration are getting much more negative according to the NatCen British Social Attitudes Survey.[71] However, graduates are four times more likely to back immigration than those with no or low qualifications are.

Stupidity is a terrible thing.

---

71 No. 31, published in June 2013.

Part III

Part III

Who dares wins

I REALISE I am trying to shout down a tornado of emotion and noise, but it is essential to turn this around for all our sakes. Most of all, it is essential for the Tory Party – which is what really concerns me. Those of us who are not caught up in the mass hysteria should speak up, lobby and use moral, economic, historical and political arguments again and again.

Here is what I mean.

Ian Birrell, the brilliant columnist and ex-deputy editor of *The Independent*, is indefatigable. He has a disabled child who has been cared for by migrants and that perhaps explains why, year on year, he writes and speaks up in favour of migration:

This is what happens when mainstream politicians fail to confront the myths and misinformation of misanthropes. This is the hideous consequence of mainstream parties spooked by UKIP and joining a bidding war to be the most hostile to immigrants instead of challenging the prejudices of a party playing on people's insecurities. This is the result of crass talk of communities being 'swamped', along with the rise in racism and religious bigotry identified by Justin Welby, the Archbishop of Canterbury. This is the legacy of lionising and ennobling a narrow-minded immigrant obsessive. This is the tragic inevitability of a politics fuelled by fear and pessimism. Britain must decide if it wants to remain an open and optimistic force in the world or curl up like a defensive hedgehog and show only prickles to the rest of the planet.[72]

Well, what do we want?

As 2015 dawned, Theresa May announced that foreign students would be 'expelled' from the UK after

---

72 *The Guardian*, 29 October 2014.

they had graduated. Here is your prickly hedgehog. Inventor Sir James Dyson slammed the plans, but the lady was not for turning. Apparently George Osborne is quashing the idea, though – and quite right, too. The US goes to India and China looking for talented young people; we throw them out after they have paid high fees to study at our universities. We tell them they are not wanted.

The issue for the Conservatives is that they will never ever get the majorities they need unless more people in the minority communities believe the party is for them. The party needs to say to each one of those voters: 'I not only admire and welcome you, I want to see you get on in a Conservative environment. I want you to have a productive, fulfilling life without fear or feeling you are damned whatever you do.' If that doesn't happen, minorities will continue to vote for Labour three to one. They think that the left is the only choice they really have. In fact, this has gone on for so long that they don't even think about it. It is a habit. Labour offers them the nice handout and the welfare state. Most immigrants have bigger ambitions than that, but they still don't trust the Tories – the party of big ambitions.

They see through the duplicities, too. Immigrants didn't get to where they are by being stupid. Tories talk about immigrants in one way and then tell settled black and Asian people that they are much loved. This just makes them sound shifty. Whenever they talk about diversity they create an uncomfortable reaction because it doesn't feel real or genuine. I mean, I wouldn't hand them my vote if I was called Mr Singh or Mr Patel.

OK, what we do have to accept is that Muslim extremists have really shaken up the faith of native Britons. I understand that. I am shocked by what they think and what they do. The murder of Lee Rigby was a terrible moment for all who support migration and equality of opportunity. But we have been here before. In the '70s and '80s, the IRA and other Irish militia killed dozens of Britons and maimed many more. Never forget that the US allowed the IRA to fundraise and build up support with impunity. But, even with all that going on, we didn't stop Irish migration and we didn't turn all Irish settlers into the enemy, guilty by association. So we must not do it to blameless Muslims either, who are even more scared of their militants than white people because they know what is at stake. We must be tough and we must always be fair. That is the British way. We were much less hysterical than the Americans after the bombings in London. That difference showed up. Why? Even the right-wing papers chose to run several pages on Islam's real messages.

But, to return to the Tory Party...

Lord Ashcroft is an astute political predictor. He sits outside the No. 10 tent but they don't like him because he is not clubbable. His polling, however, has clearly shown that even third-generation migrants feel they have no other choice but Labour; that they can't really trust the Tory Party. Even worse, they feel they are still unknown 'aliens' in the Tory consciousness – imagined, nightmarish creatures from another planet.

Now, if this were any other policy problem, the smart guys from the party would have gone into overdrive and solved it. So why haven't they tackled this serious obstacle to victory? Because they are not racist in the accepted 'I don't like you because of the colour of your skin' sense, but rather in the political sense. They think they will lose votes by embracing people of a different colour and that they should instead become a genuine, respectable alternative to UKIP. I say they are looking at the problem the wrong way.

Think of the population, the demographics. There are two sides to this.

We are a small island with a big population and that needs to be acknowledged. However, there is absolutely no need to talk about the population numbers in racial terms. The Tories are missing an opportunity, perhaps forever. The reality will sting their eyes. They are cutting their own throats and they will not win the next election outright. Why? Look at previous results in every town and city that has minorities. As Ashcroft has repeatedly shown, Tories need to change their image, their talk and their inwardness and attract the non-white vote. Theresa May said in 2002: 'There is a lot we need to do in this party of ours. Our base is too narrow and so, occasionally, are our sympathies. You know some people call us "the nasty party".' Well, the party has just got nastier and nastier and she is a senior member of its front bench.

These days her expressed views and policies on migration show just how much she has moved away from the woman she seemed to be twelve years ago. One wonders if it's the wine they drink that makes these Tories lose direction and all good sense.

So, what about the UKIP effect? It cannot be denied. It has traction and is changing the shape of politics in Britain, though I still think it is a blip. But I am not an elected politician so I am not as anxious as the Tories must be. They have to respond to this swell and surge, but they need to hold their nerve too and remain clear-headed. Some of their MPs are jumping ship and going off to join UKIP, only to survive as MPs because they don't really believe any of the UKIP rubbish. Conservative voters and backers are moving too, though. It happens. Labour suffered that indignity when Shirley Williams, Roy Jenkins and others broke off from the too-lefty Labour Party to form the Social Democratic Party. By the way, where is the SDP now? It lasted from 1981 to 1987. A full seven years. After all that fanfare, they went off and became the rump of the Liberals. Remember also that, not too long ago, many serious commentators and political leaders feared the British National Party was going to become a force to be reckoned with. Where are they now? So yes, UKIP cannot be ignored, but it can't hold the flame of British politics either. It can't lead the way or determine the future of this nation. Many are indeed fruitcakes, loonies and closet racists, as Cameron famously described them in 2006.[73] The Tories who vote for UKIP are old, disenchanted and unsettled in the modern world, but I don't see university students queuing up to join them.

It is important for all of us who are not seduced or frightened by these Johnny-come-latelies to stay steady and keep our sanity. Britons are centrists by nature. They flirt with extremes but in the end they come back to the centre. Millions are also naturally conservative – mistrustful of revolutions and radical changes.

Remember that, at present, Labour are vulnerable too. They are trying to dupe everybody, but, in a sense, the Tories have the chance to gain an advantage. Miliband, the cunning little fox, is trying to turn both ways. He

73 He said this on LBC on 4 April 2006.

doesn't want to lose the traditional, white, working-class supporters – many of whom are grumpy and going off to UKIP these days – but he also wants to hold on to the minority votes, which keep coming in by the bucketful, as usual. He says more must be done to reduce migration and then he speaks warm words to his black and Asian supporters so they don't feel threatened. It is actually rather disgraceful how he is playing this. Everyone who has a brain knows what the game is.

And then there's the wretched third party of British politics – losers every one of them. Let's face it, the Lib Dems are a white party – even more white and closed-off than the Tories. In 2014, at their party conference in Glasgow, you saw hardly any people of colour. It was like landing in the North Pole: white – white everywhere (except, of course, for the cleaners and servers – the unseen hands making it all run smoothly). Well, the party is on its way into the graveyard of history, which makes things even more urgent for the Tories. They must step up – and fast.

They need to be clear and announce straight, honest policy options. They need to say to minorities:

> We know most of you work all hours and your families
> do that too. We know how enterprising you are when you
> find it hard to get bank loans and extra capital. You raise
> money through your networks; you are not defeated by
> the system. You belong in this party and you will find
> this is your party, with family values and enterprise at
> the heart of it.

They can't just *say* this, though – they have got to mean
it. They also need to make it clear that they will never
patronise minorities, offer them a special status or pre-
ferment, or push them ahead because it is assumed they
can't do it on their own merits. 'Yes, you can!' should
be their message.

I talked to some Indian and Chinese business people and their high-flying children. They all vote Labour.
Why? Well, the Chinese men – all five of them – said
that they felt a historical obligation to vote for the party:

> That is what my father did when he came from Hong
> Kong. He didn't like Mrs Thatcher and what she said
> about us swamping British culture. So it just became a

family tradition. You know, we Chinese are very traditional. But anyway, show me what the Conservative
Party is doing to invite the Chinese in. I can't see anything. We are proud people. We do not go where we
are not wanted.

His son, a dentist, agreed: 'Maybe now, Labour, they
take us for granted. But at the party conference this
year I saw many young British Chinese people there,
so they are renewing the connection.' The children in
these families are successful entrepreneurs but also doctors, dentists, financial whizzos, managers and investors.
Some of them have become go-betweens for British and
Chinese firms, being bilingual and bicultural. The Chinese are self-reliant. They believe in a small state, low
taxes and looking after each other rather than depend-
ing on benefits (unless they absolutely have to). But this
government is restricting visas for Chinese restaurant
workers; it seems not to appreciate their contributions.
Here are natural-born Tories who won't vote for the
Tory Party. What a waste.

Older Indians, Pakistanis and some Africans have a

strong and meaningful connection to the Labour Party. Many of them have been, or are, Labour councillors, and some of them personally know Jack Straw, Harriet Harman, Clare Short and so on. I mean, how many Tories are known that well by minorities? This is political capital unused by the Tories.

The younger generations in the minority communities are savvy, linked-up on the web and sophisticated. They are not necessarily committed to any one party. This is something the Tories need to understand. They have a way in like they never did before. And they are frankly screwing the chances they have. One young man, Sadiq Khan (no, not the Labour Party frontbencher), told me this:

> My father was a grocer. He came from Pakistan and worked every hour, every day, all his life 'til he dropped dead. He felt safe voting for Labour because all other Pakistanis did. I work for a big international pharmaceutical company, travel the world and have made more money than my poor father ever imagined was possible. I want to make up my own mind about whom I vote for.

So I looked at the choices. You know, I am free of the colonial relationship, that strange humility that subjects felt long after independence. So I am not grateful for small favours and will not be used by Labour. The Lib Dems seem uninterested in someone like me and the Tories either ignore us or seem to hate us. So I will not vote in 2015. This seems the only choice open to me – a high-achieving, independent and proud British Asian man.

I mean, how can this be? How do the Tories not see what they have done? Before it is too late they need to say – *must* say – to men and women like Sadiq: 'You are one of us. We are all equal. There will never be a time when we are not equal. We are grateful for the contributions your people have made to this country. Come in. You will not be disappointed.'

It is time for the UK as a country to acknowledge these contributions, too. We expect immigrants to be grateful to us for getting the chance to make new lives here. We need to return the favour and say we too are grateful for all they have done to keep the country economically and culturally strong.

What have immigrants ever done for us? Stupid question. The next time you see migrant street and office cleaners or petrol station and supermarket staff, when you are treated by a foreign-born doctor and dentist or served coffee and a panini by hard workers from eastern Europe, think of how life would be without them. And then thank them.

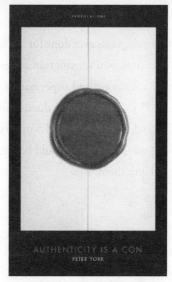

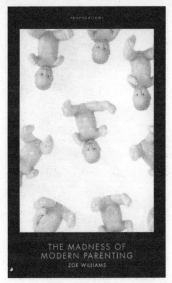